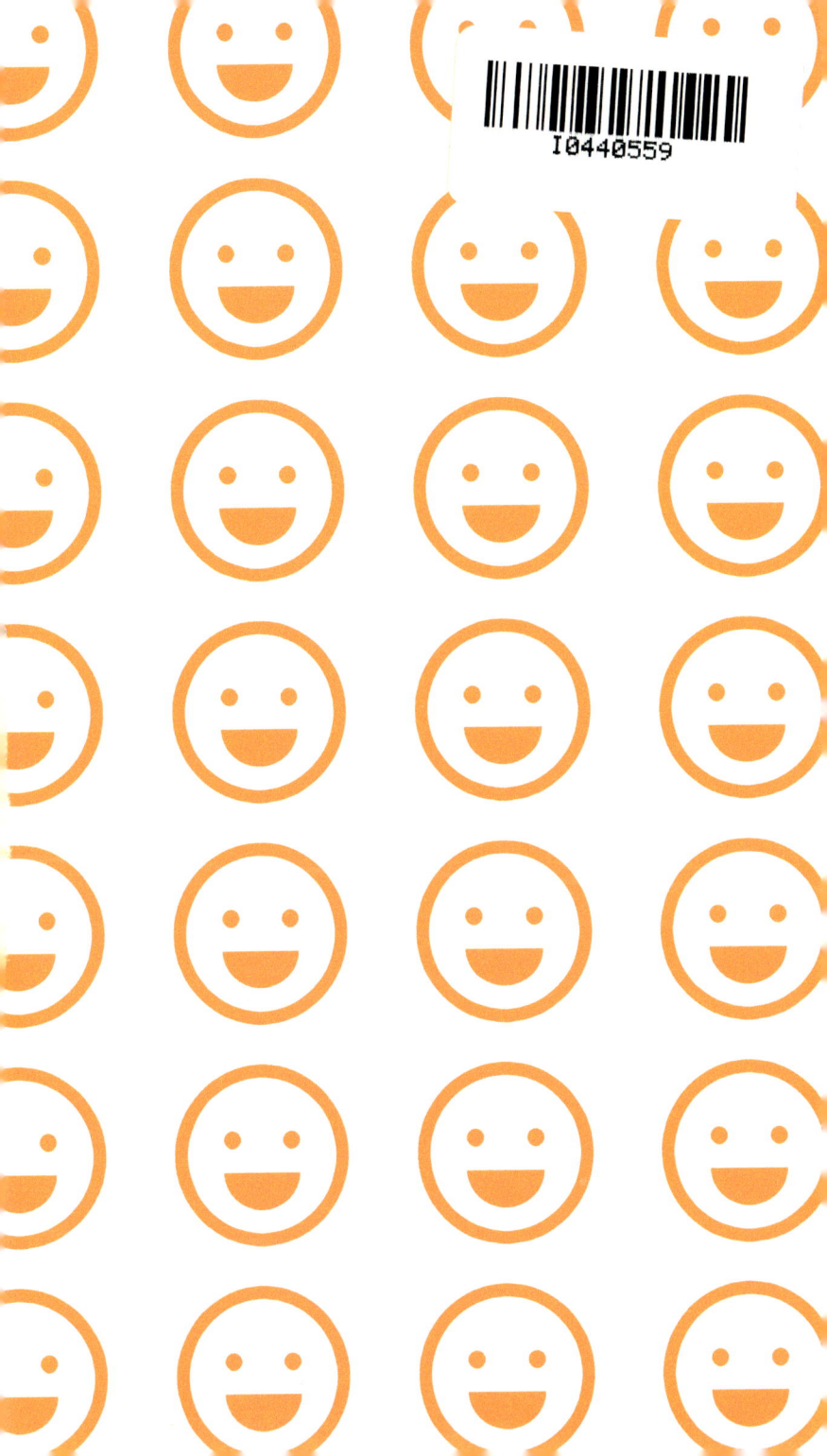

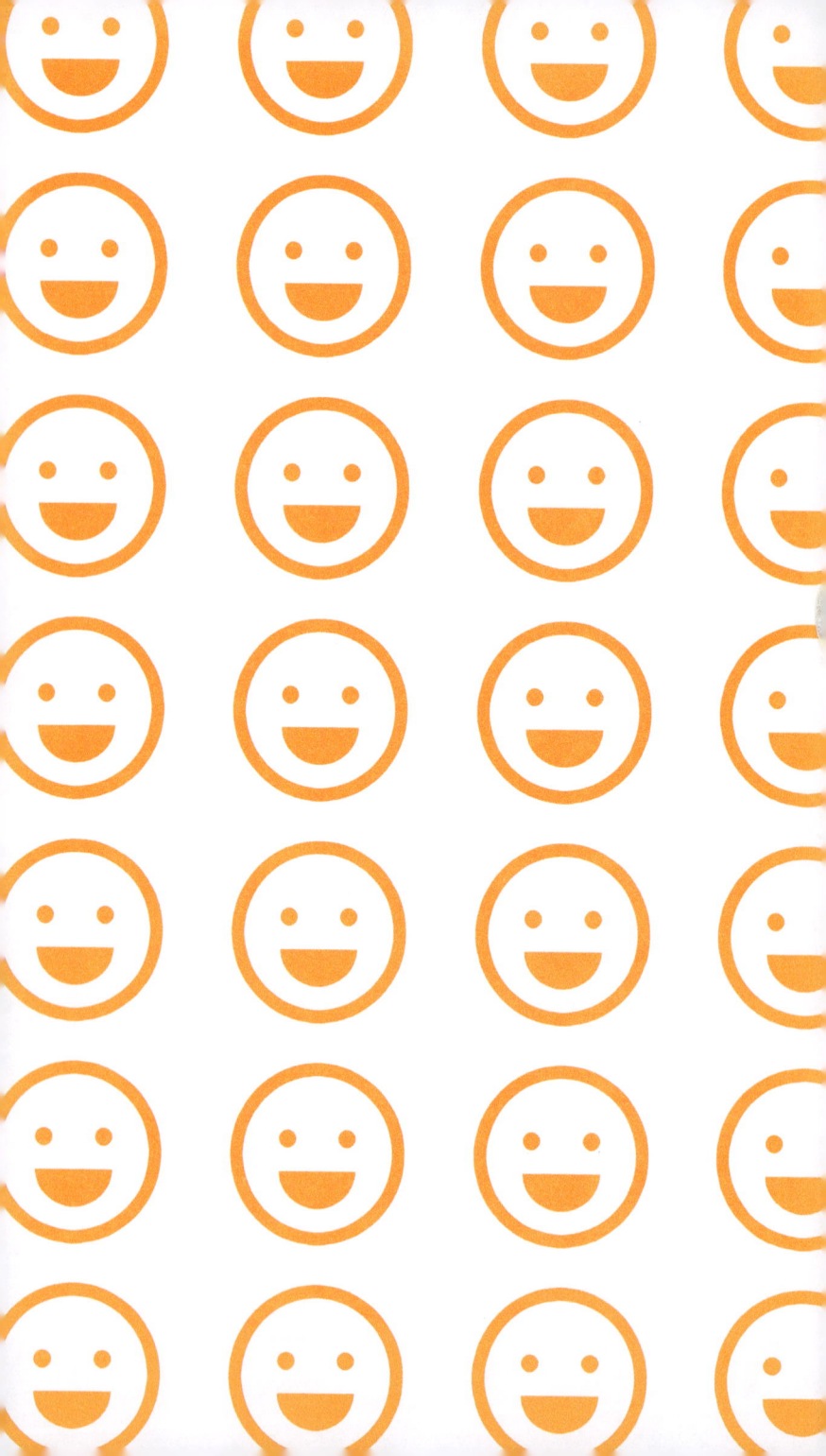

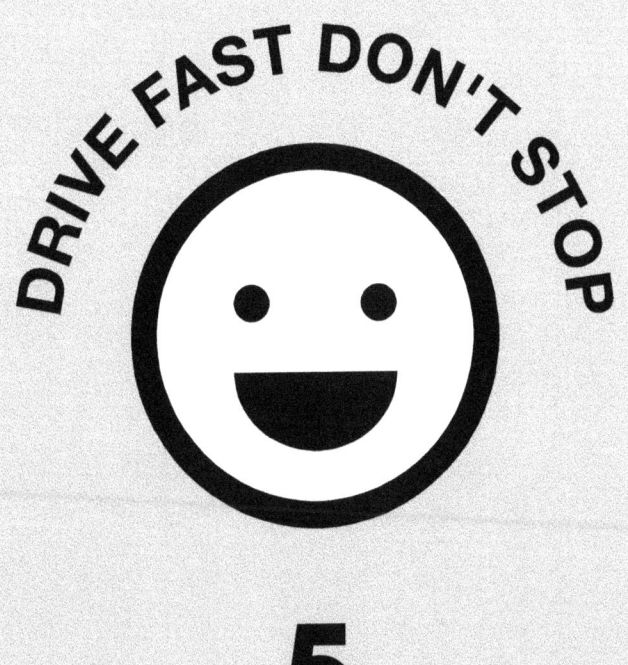

5

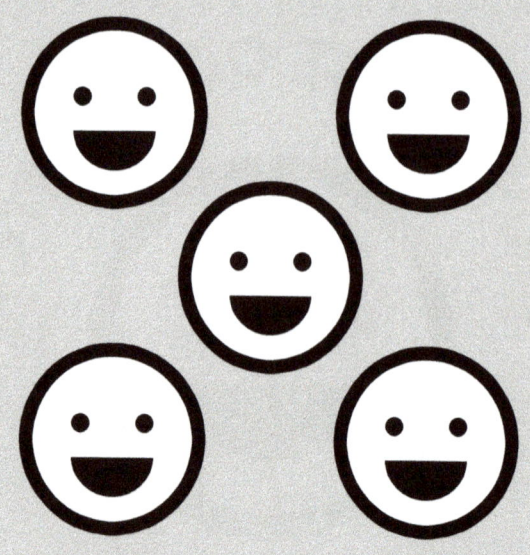

DRIVE FAST DON'T STOP

BOOK FIVE

THE RACE OF GENTLEMEN

FAST DON'T

FAST DON'T

E FAST DON'T

VE FAST DON'T ST

RIVE FAST DON'T STO

DRIVE FAST DON'T STOP

DRIVE FAST DON'T STOP

DRIVE FAST DON'T STOP

THE RACE OF GENTLEMEN

E RACE OF GENTLEM

RACE OF GENTLE

ACE OF GENTL

CE OF GENT

CE OF GEN

RACING

RACING

RACING

RACING

RACING

RACING

RACING

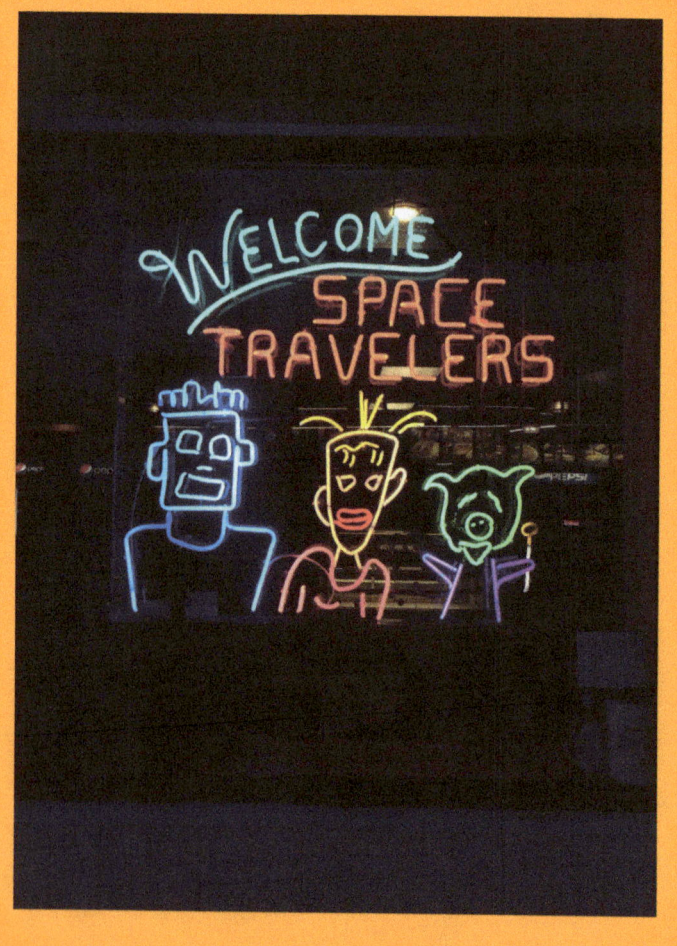

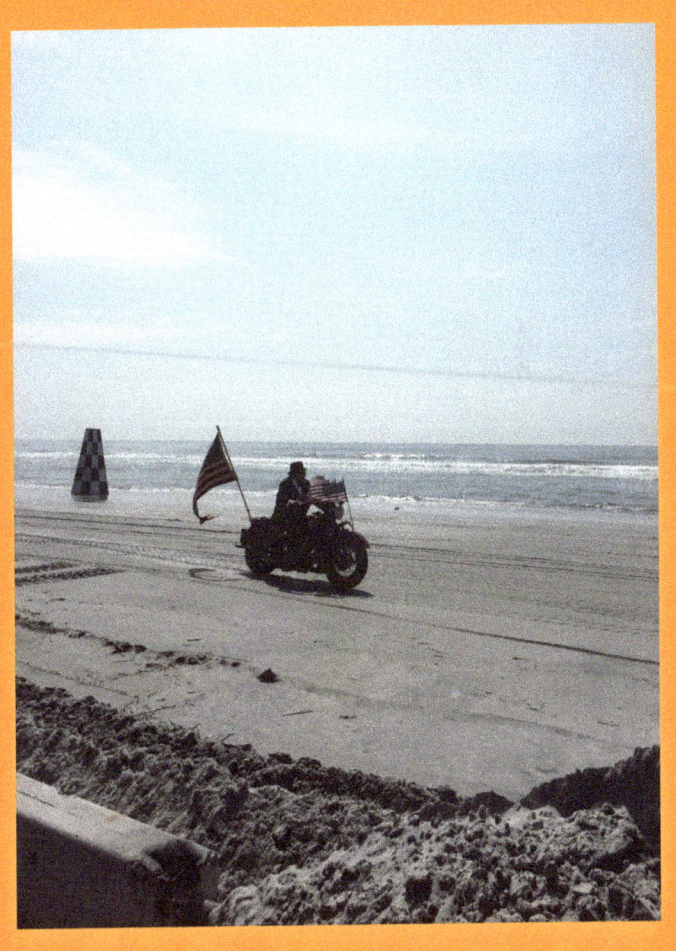

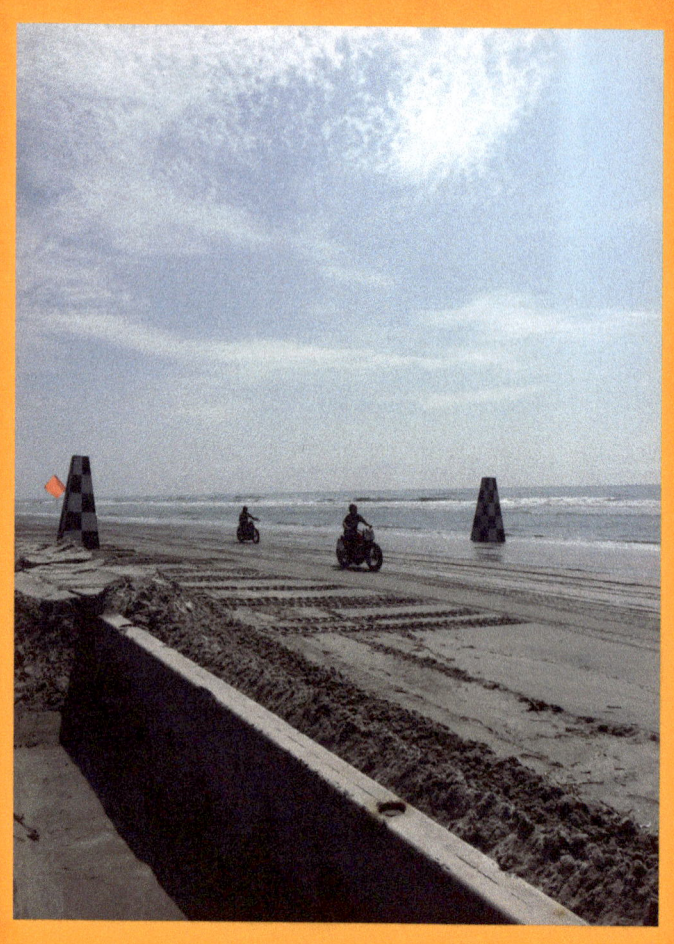

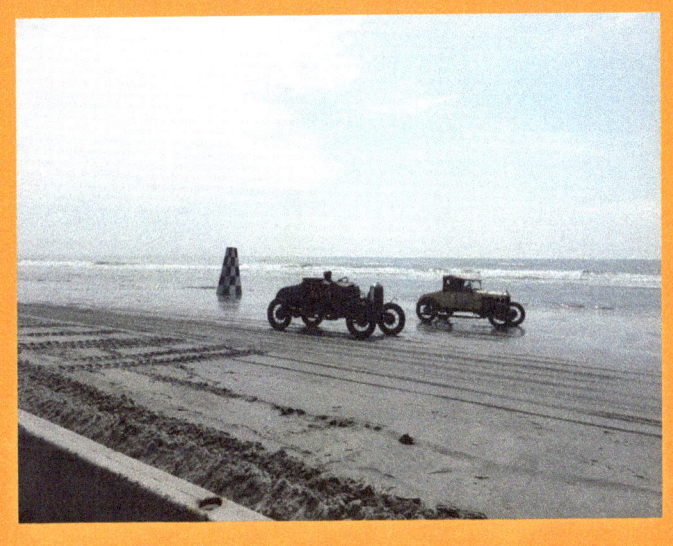

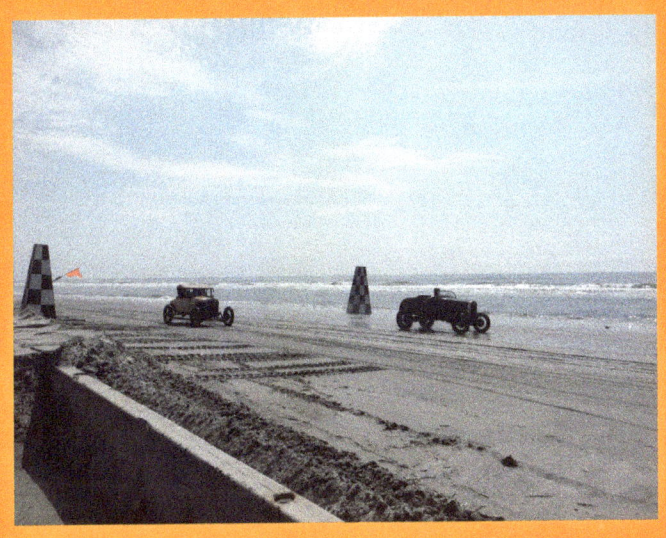

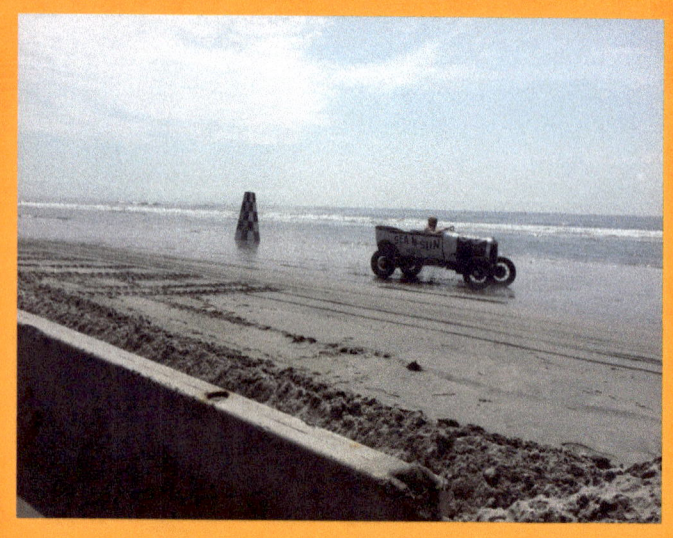

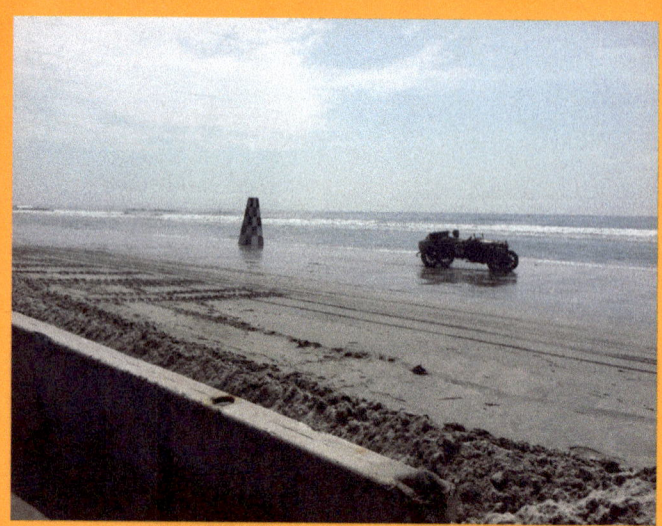

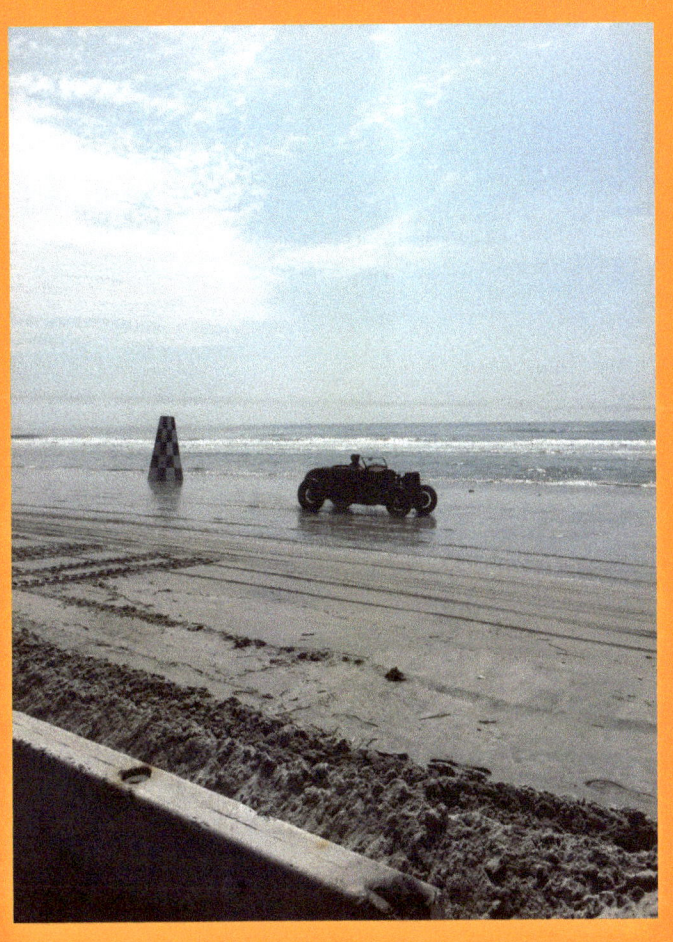

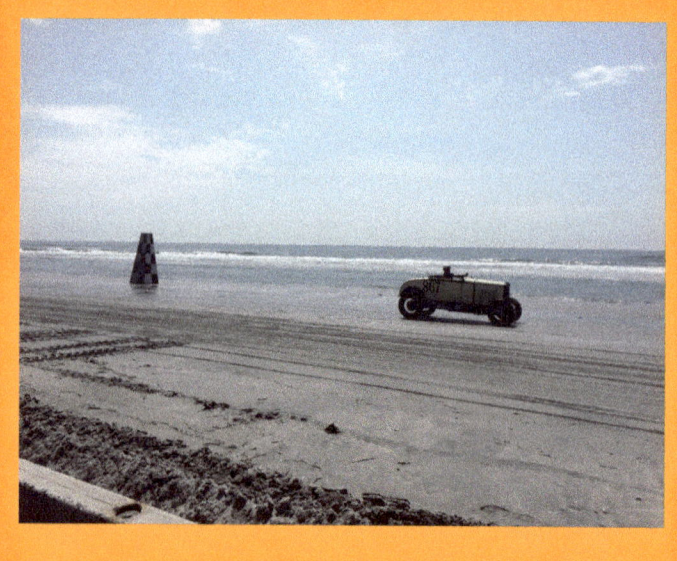

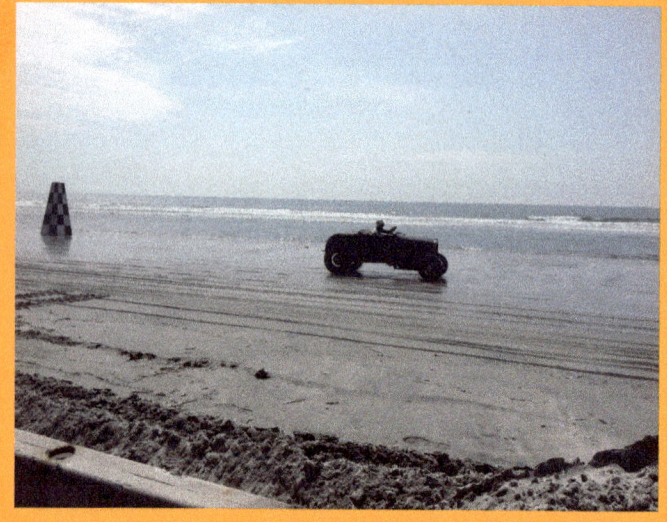

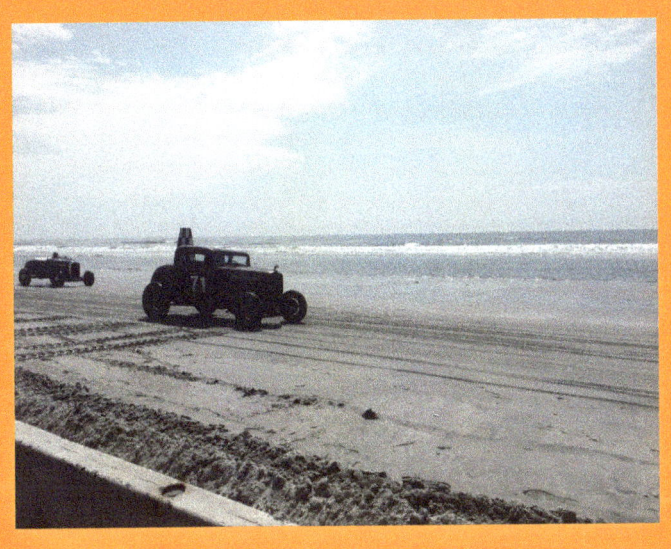

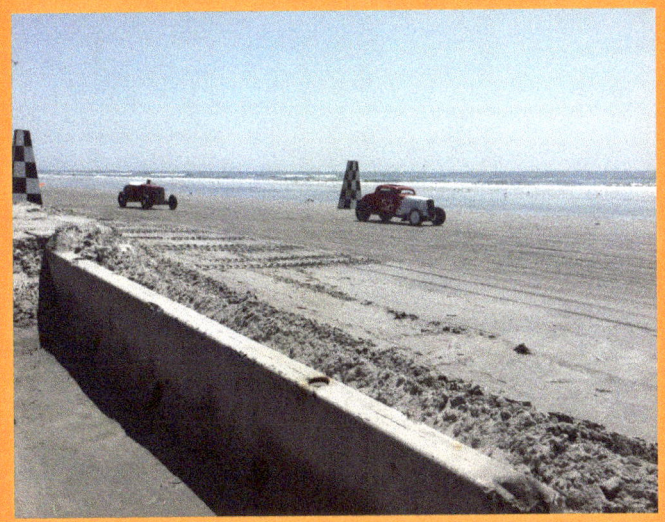

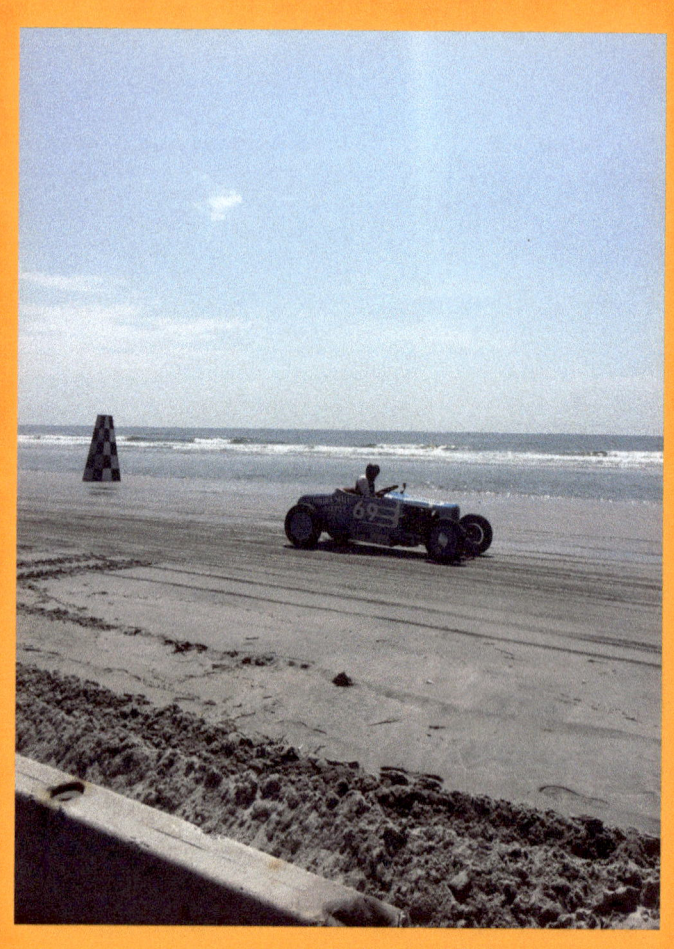

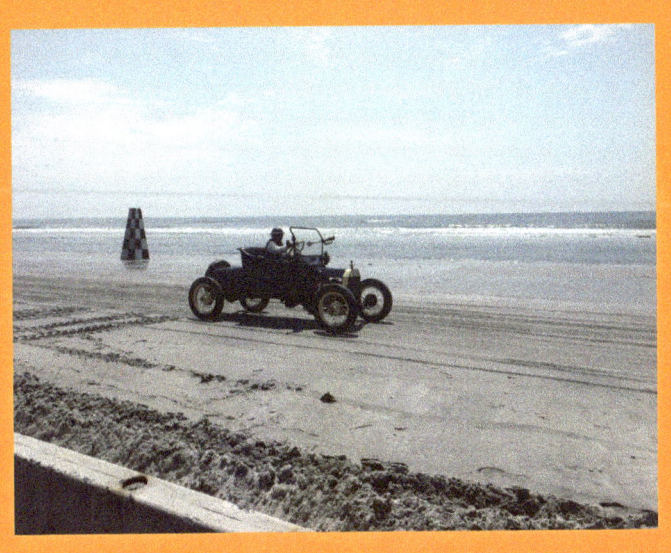

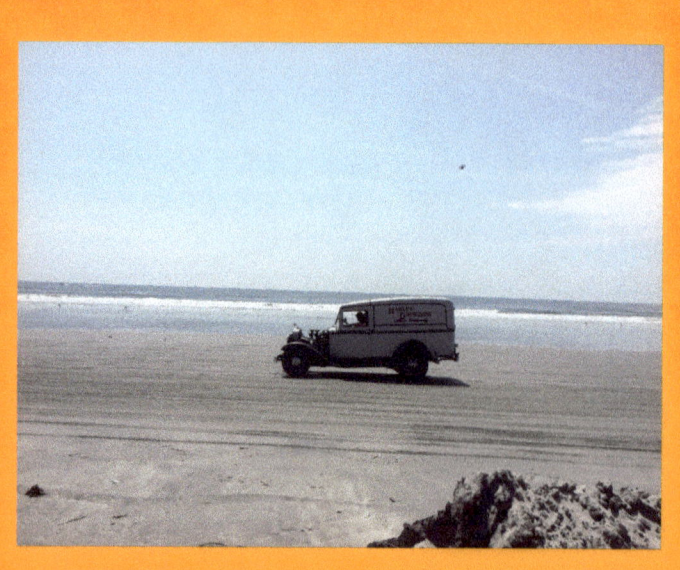

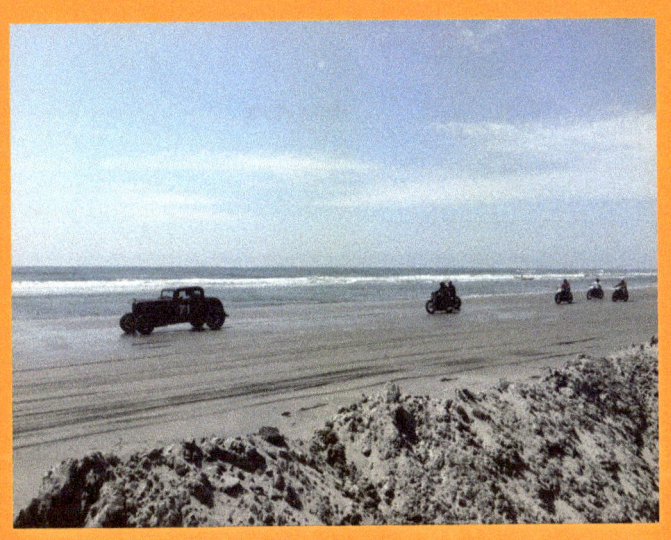

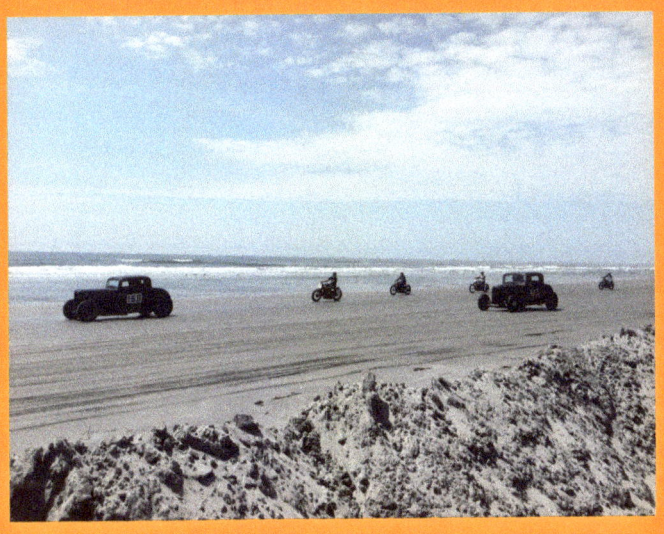

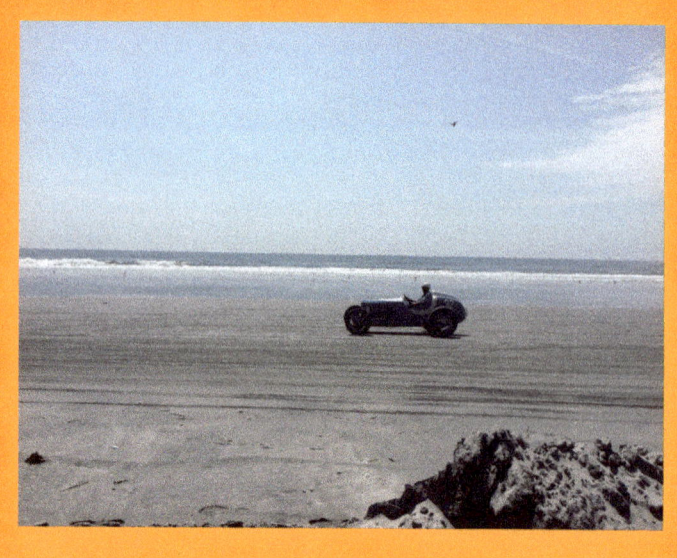

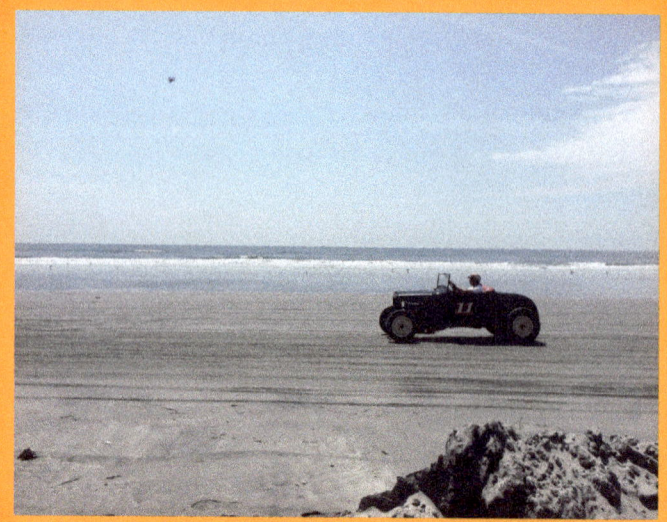

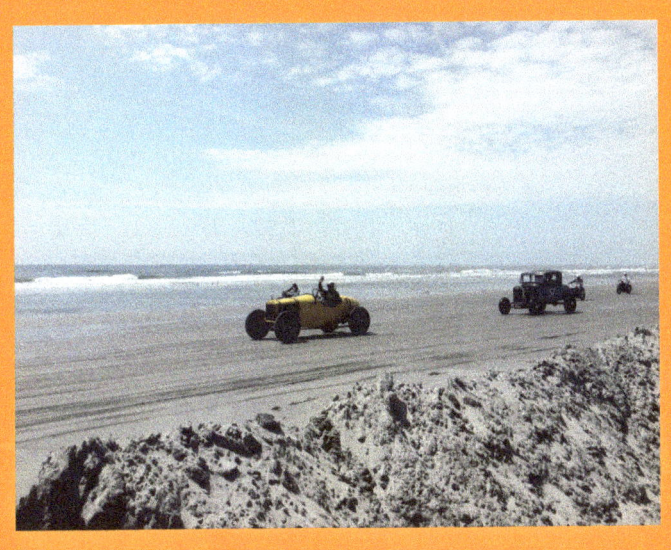

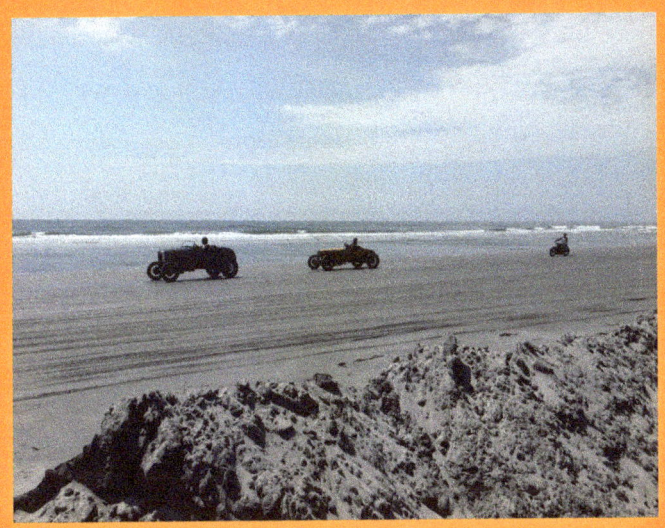

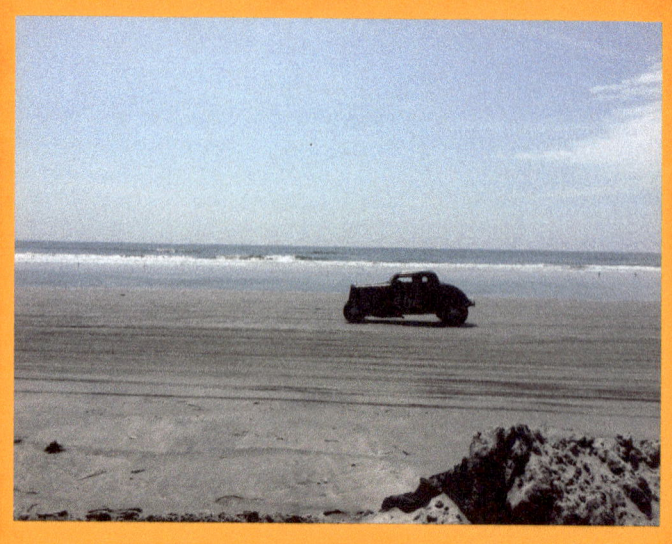

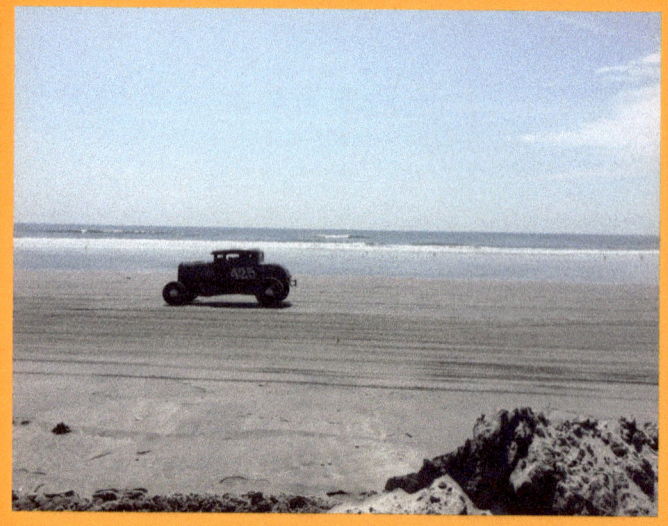

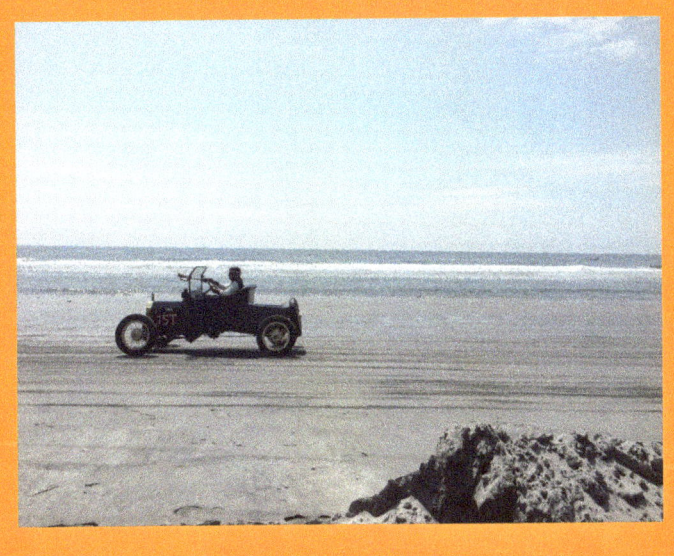

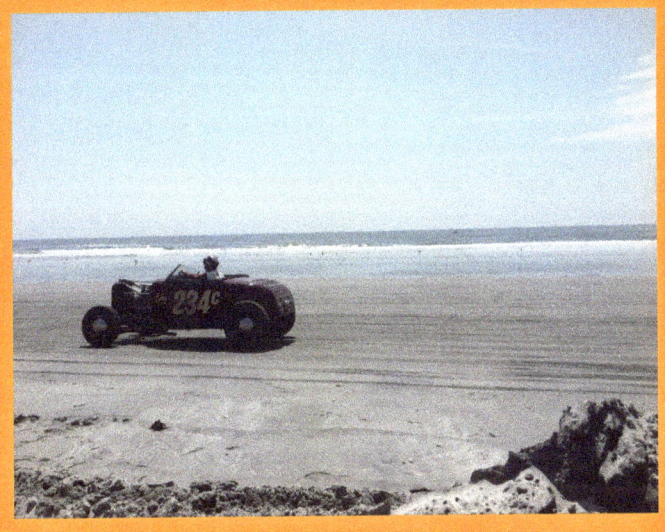

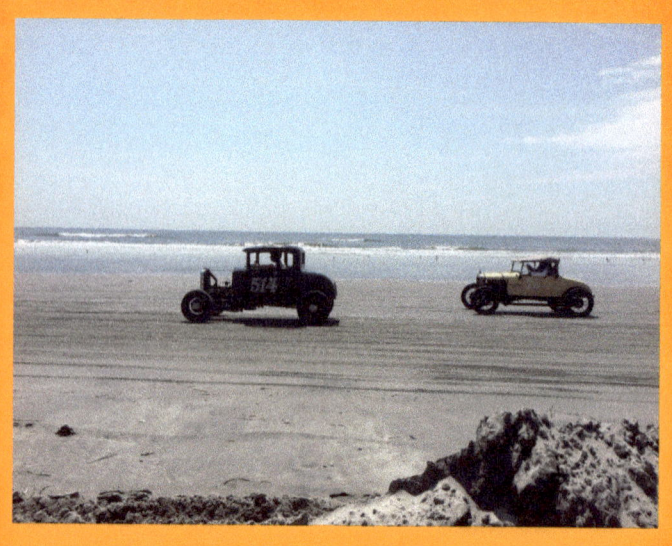

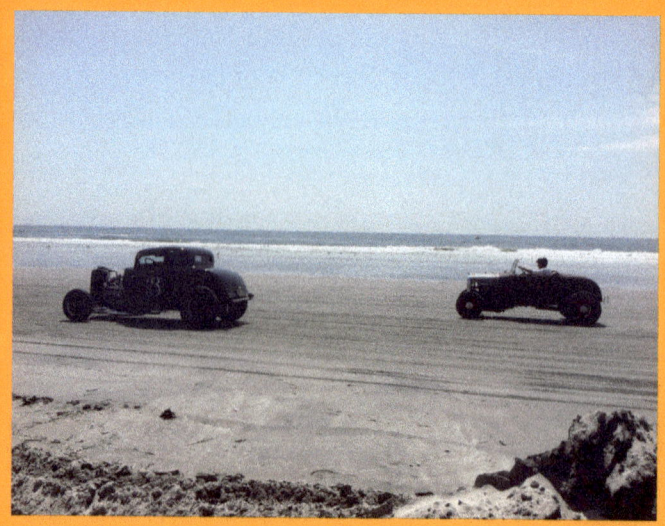

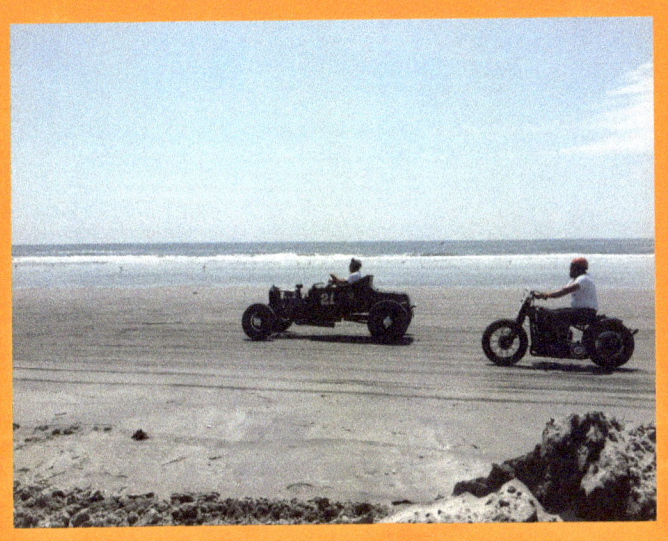

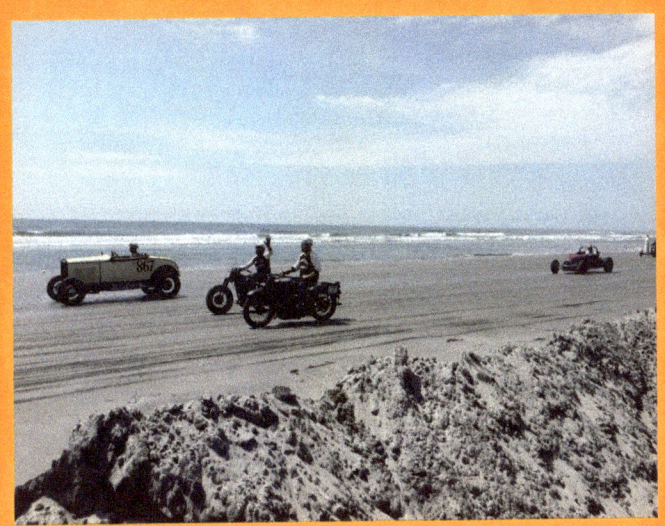

CE OF GEN

ACE OF GENT

ACE OF GENT

RACE OF GENTL

E RACE OF GENTLEM

THE RACE OF GENTLEMEN

THE RACE OF GENTLEMEN

PARKED

PARKED

PARKED

PARKED

PARKED

PARKED

PARKED

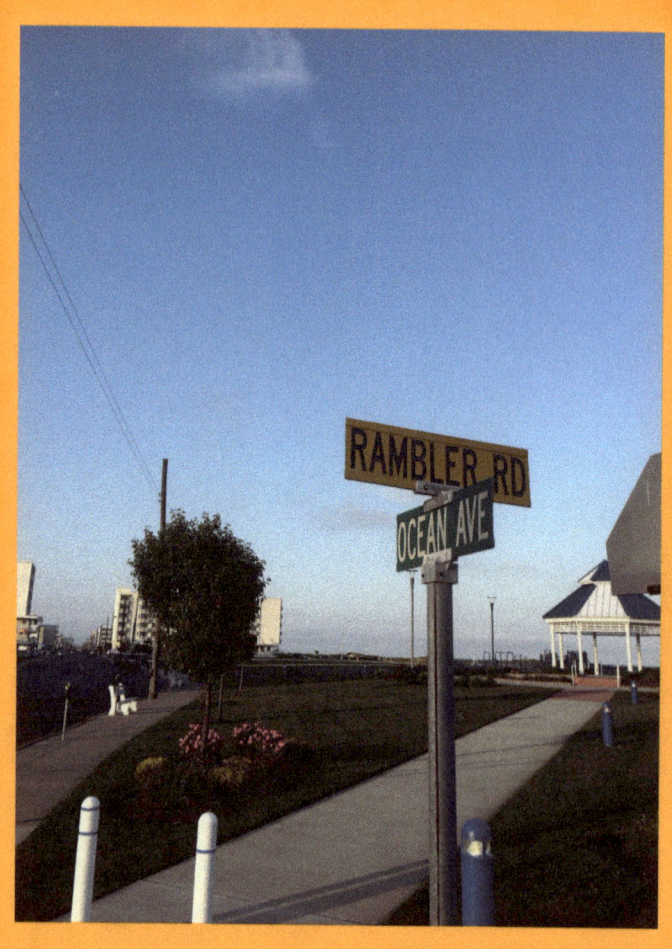

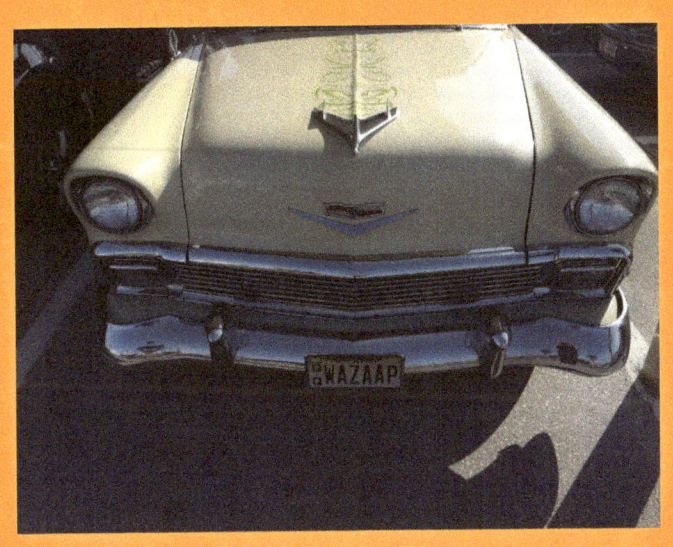

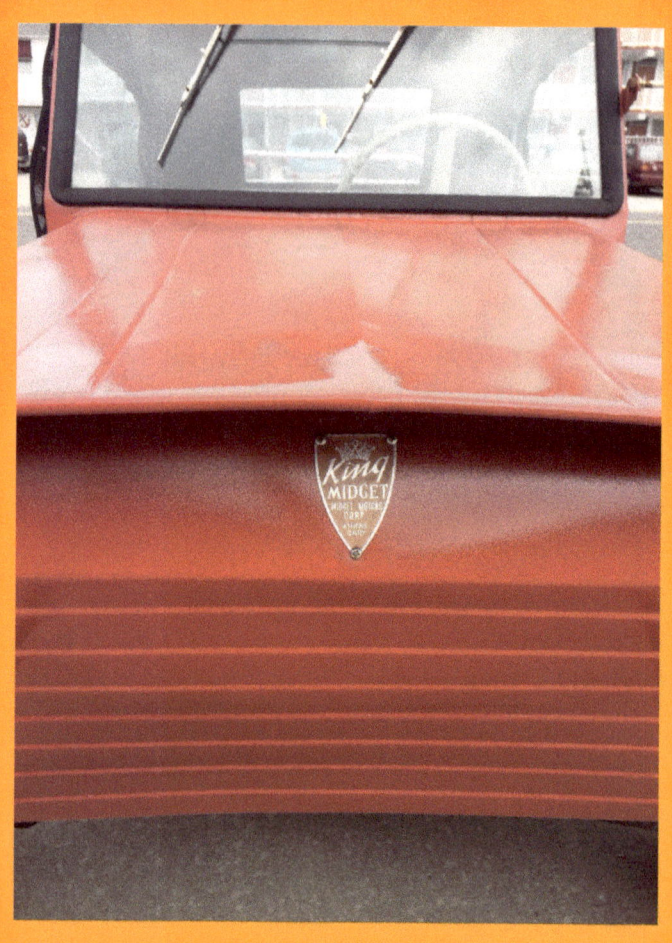

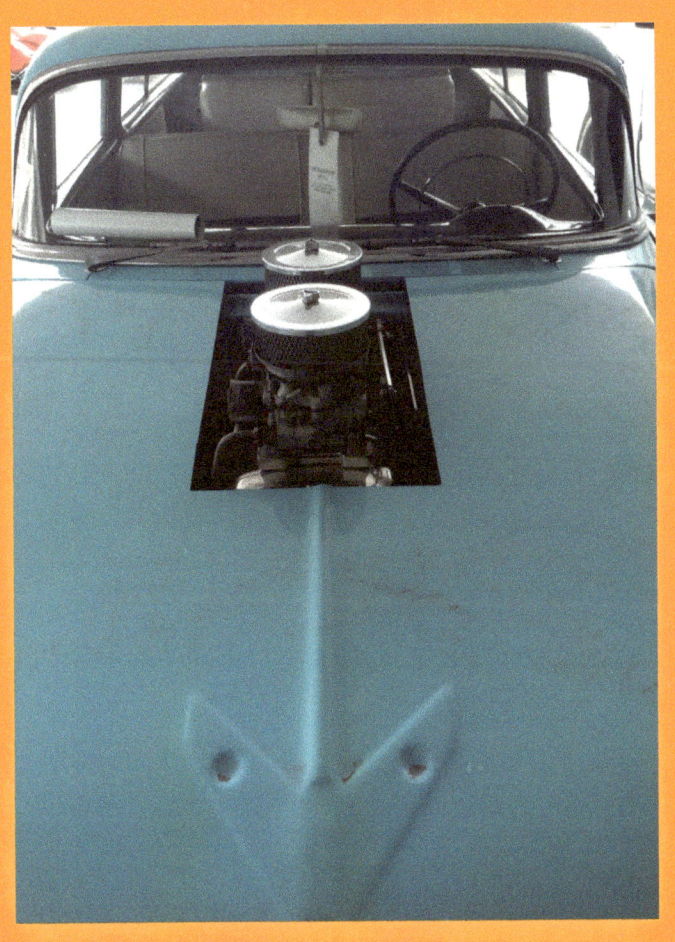

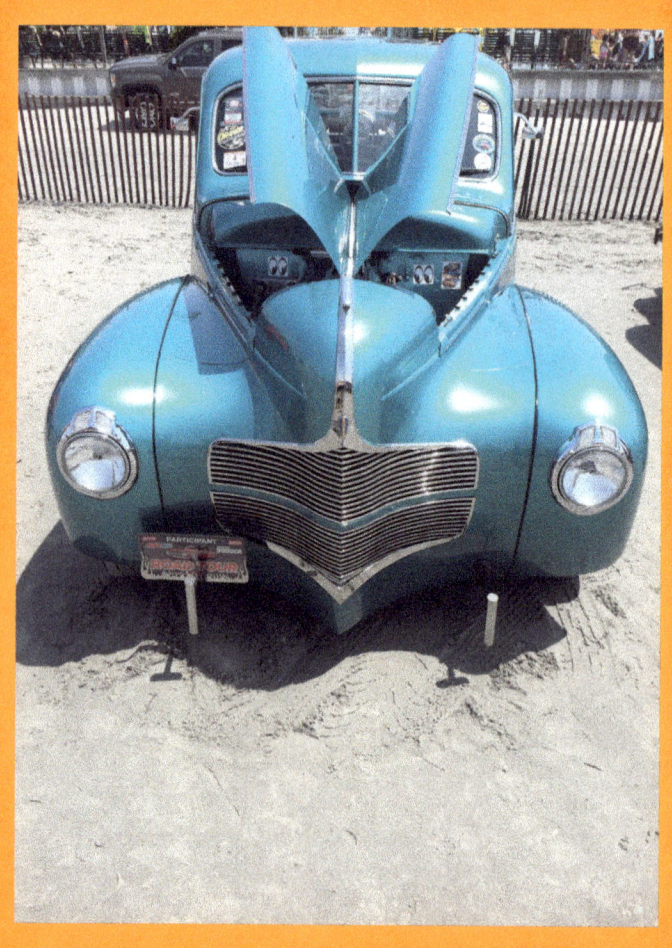

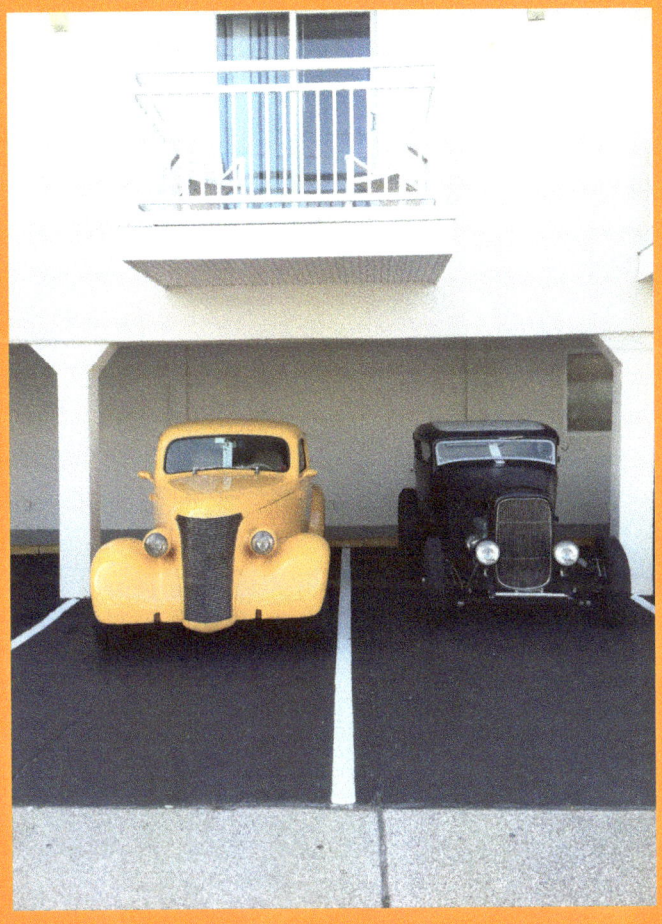

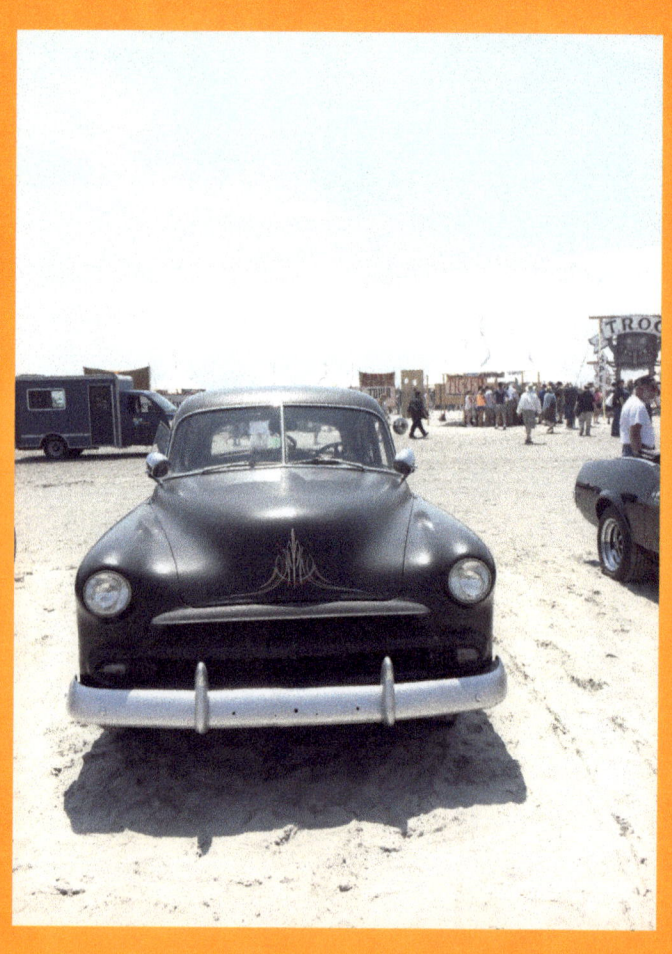

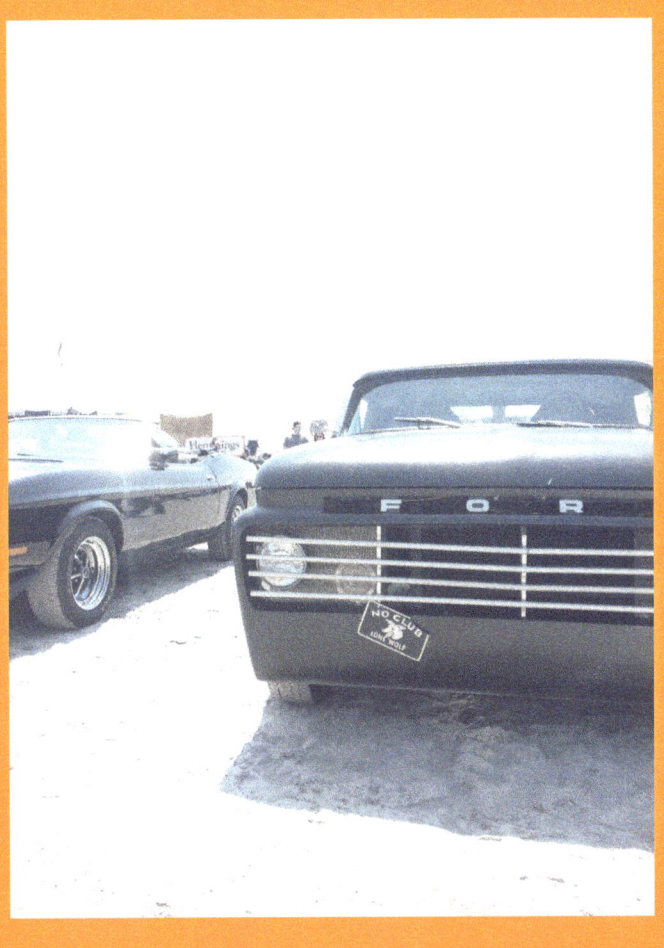

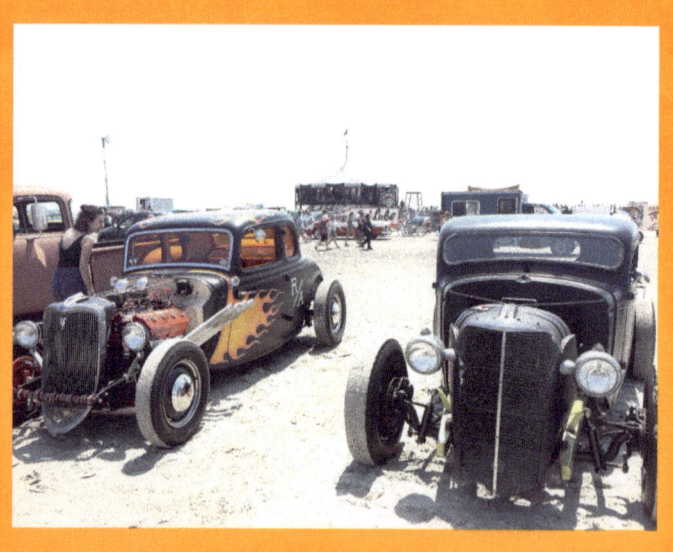

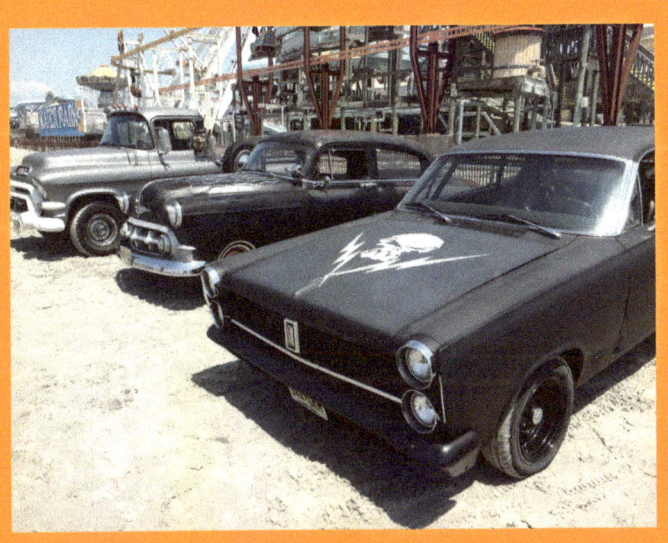

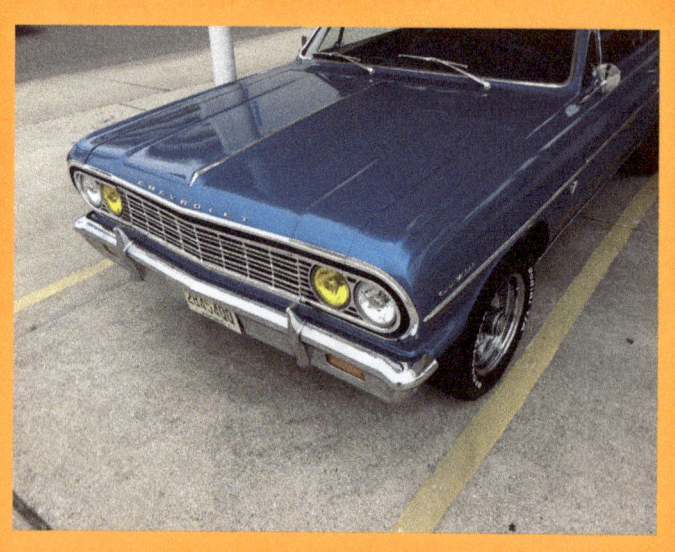

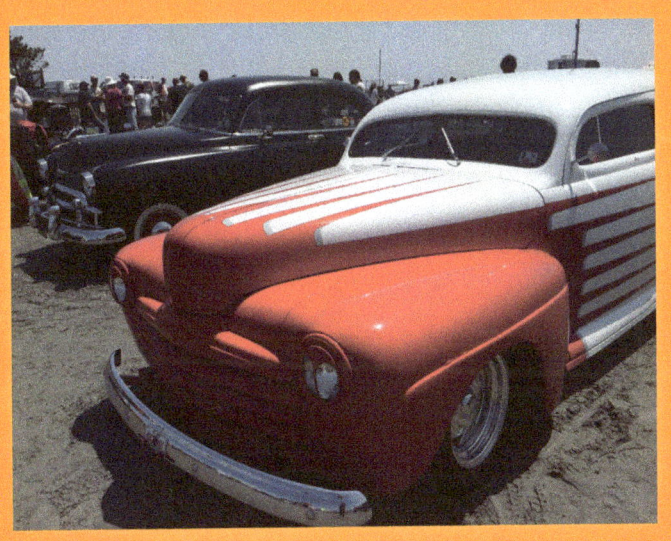

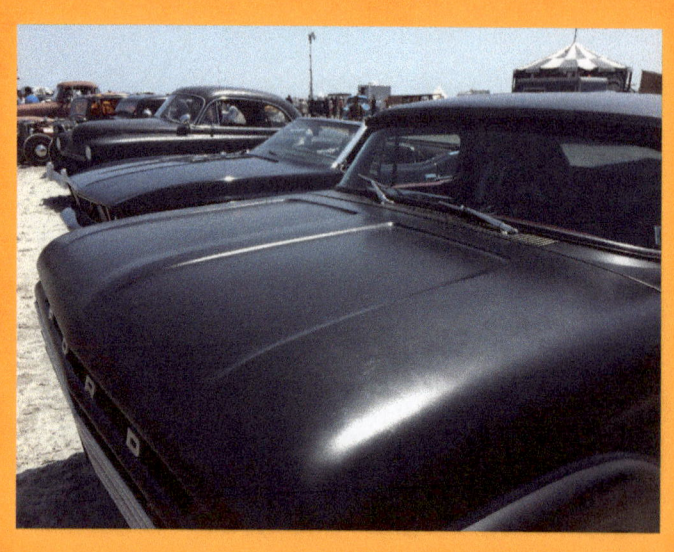

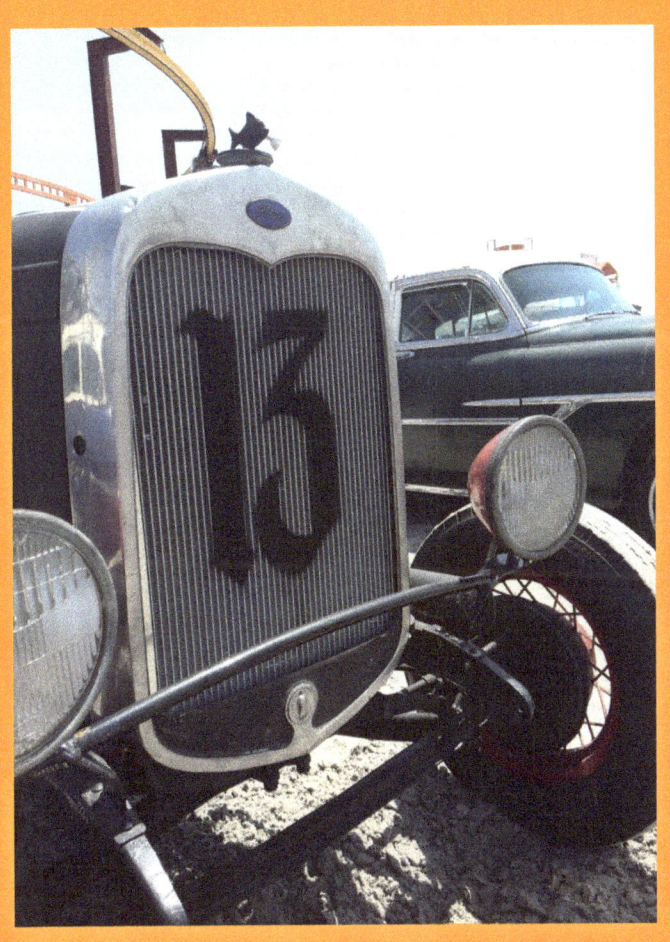

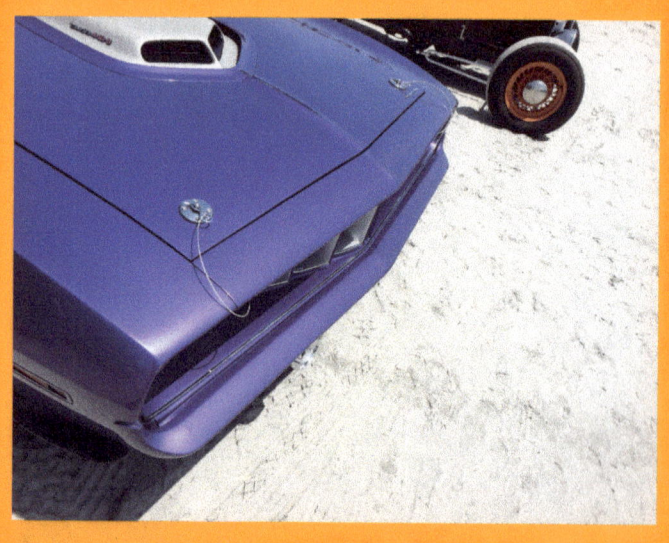

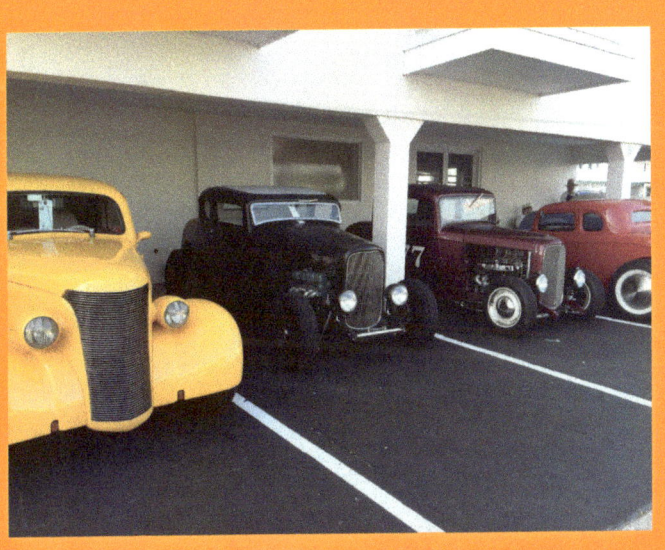

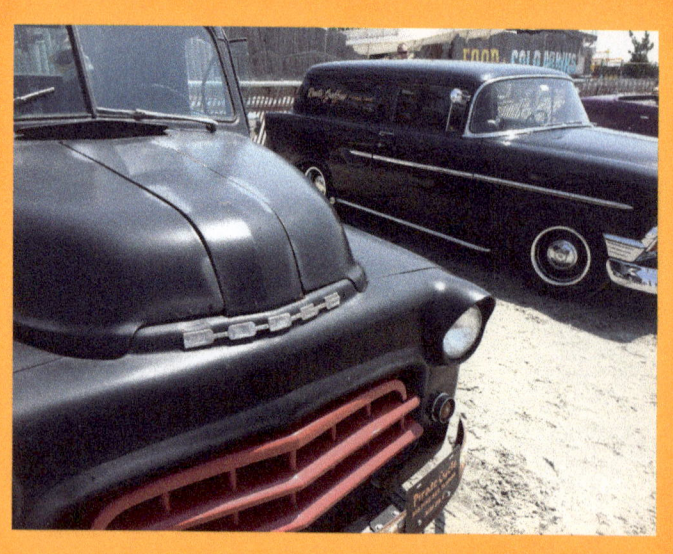

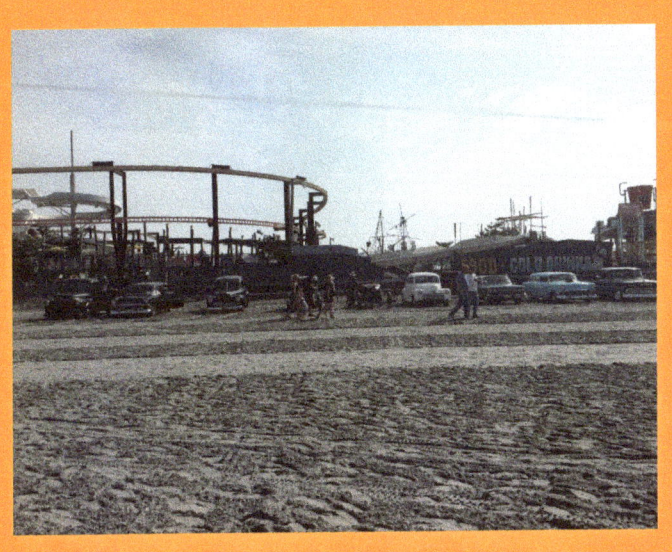

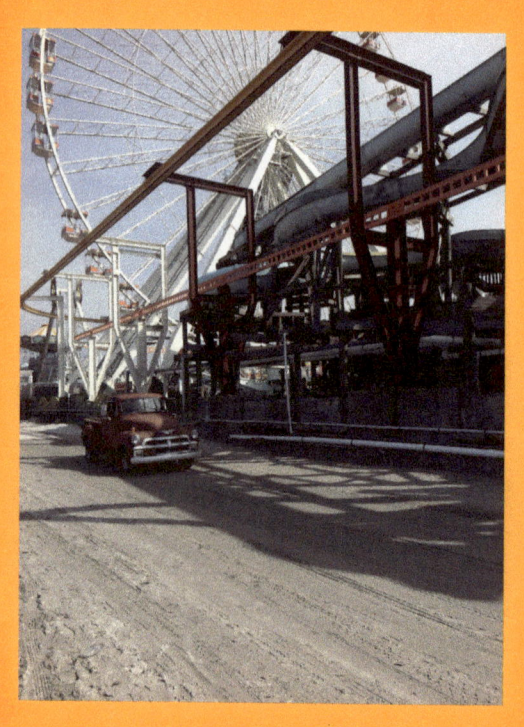

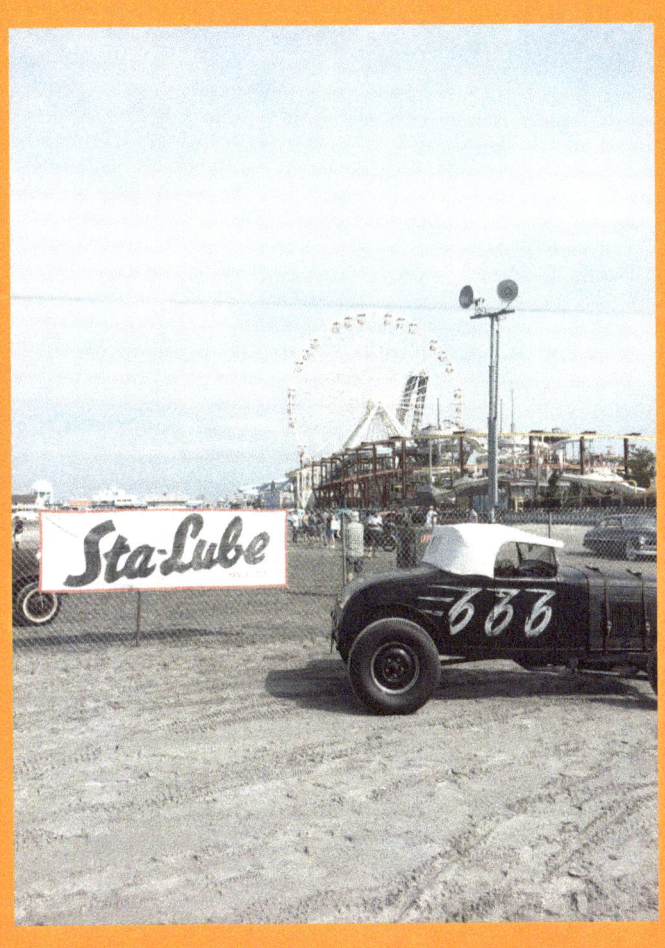

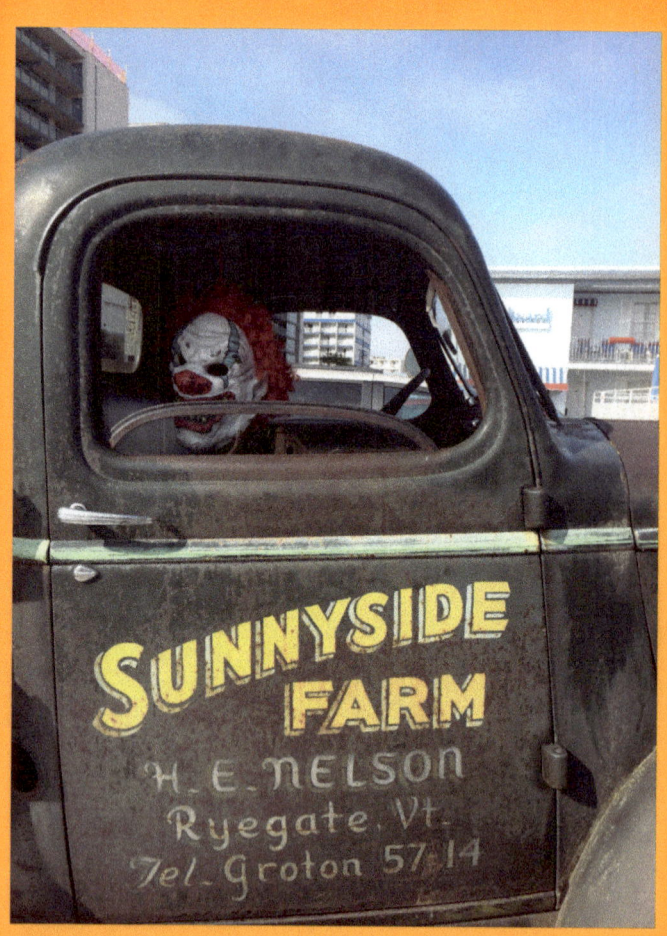

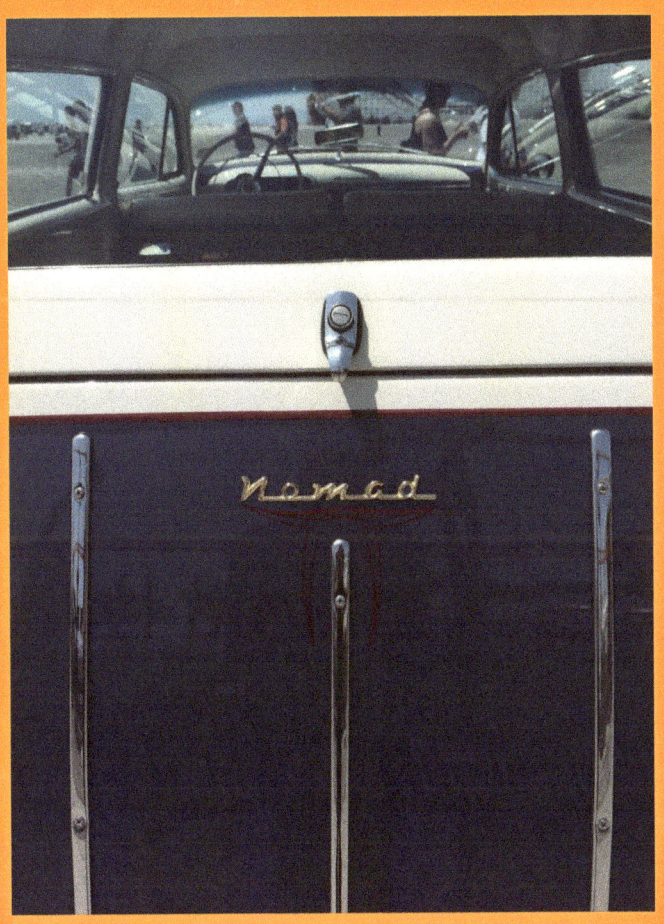

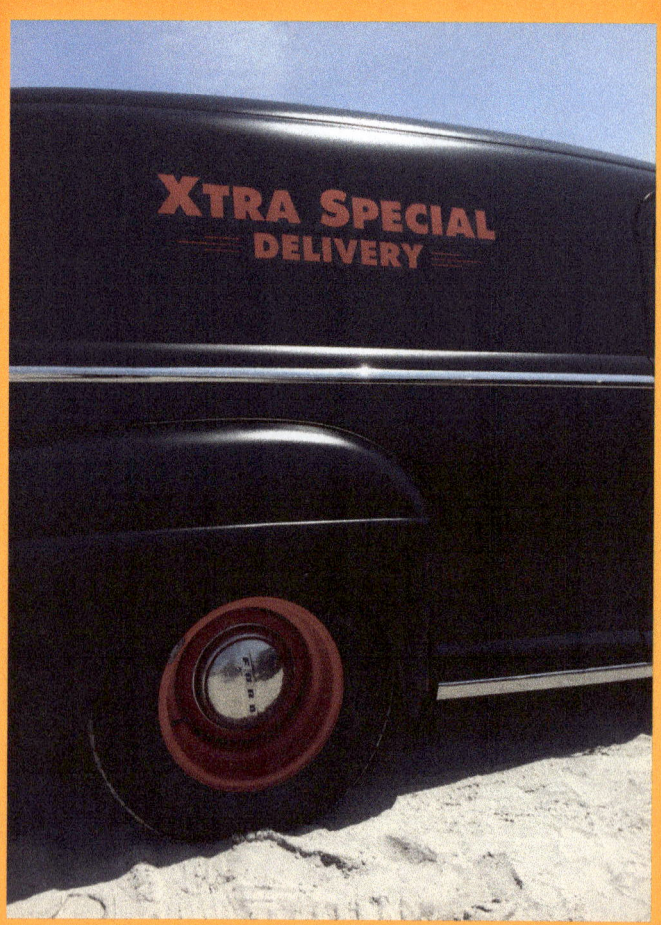

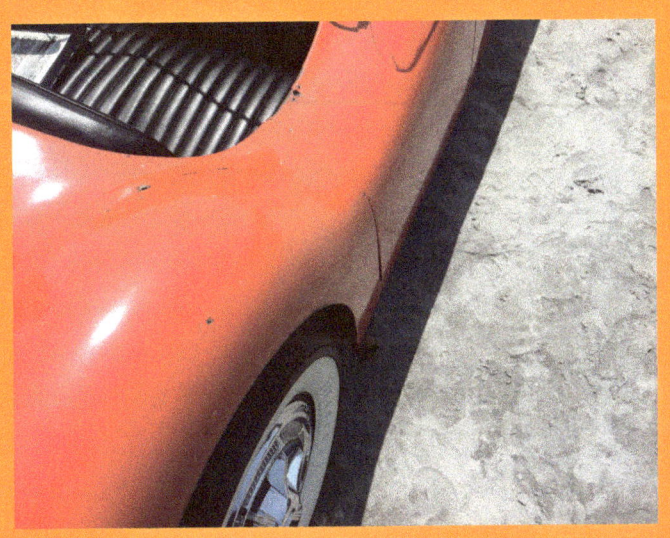

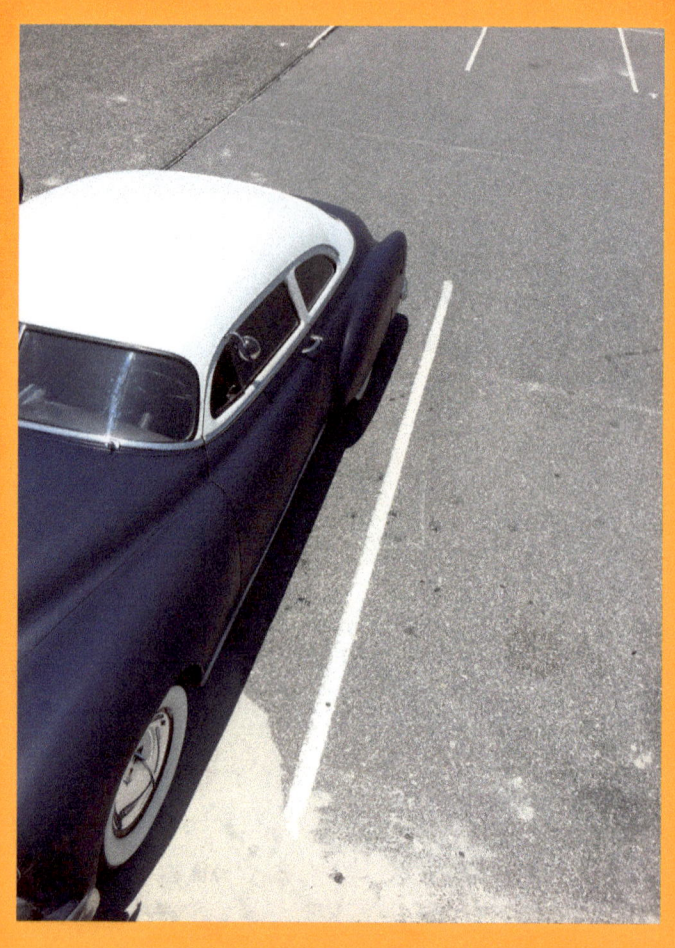

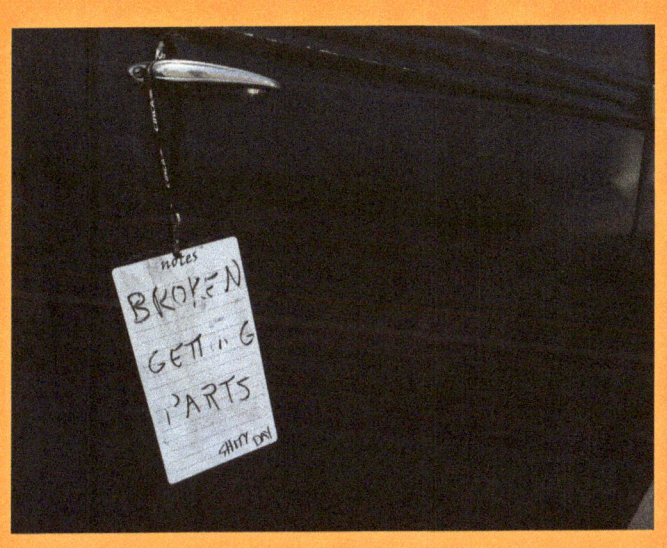

END

END

END

END

END

END

END

FAST DON'T

FAST DON'T

FAST DON'T

E FAST DON'T ST

IVE FAST DON'T STO

DRIVE FAST DON'T STOP

DRIVE FAST DON'T STOP

DRIVE FAST DON'T STOP

DRIVE FAST DON'T STOP

AUTOMOTIVE PHOTO ARCHIVE
BY
MATTHEW JOCELYN

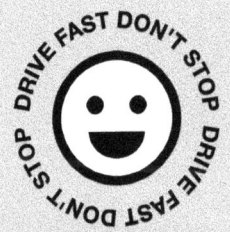

5

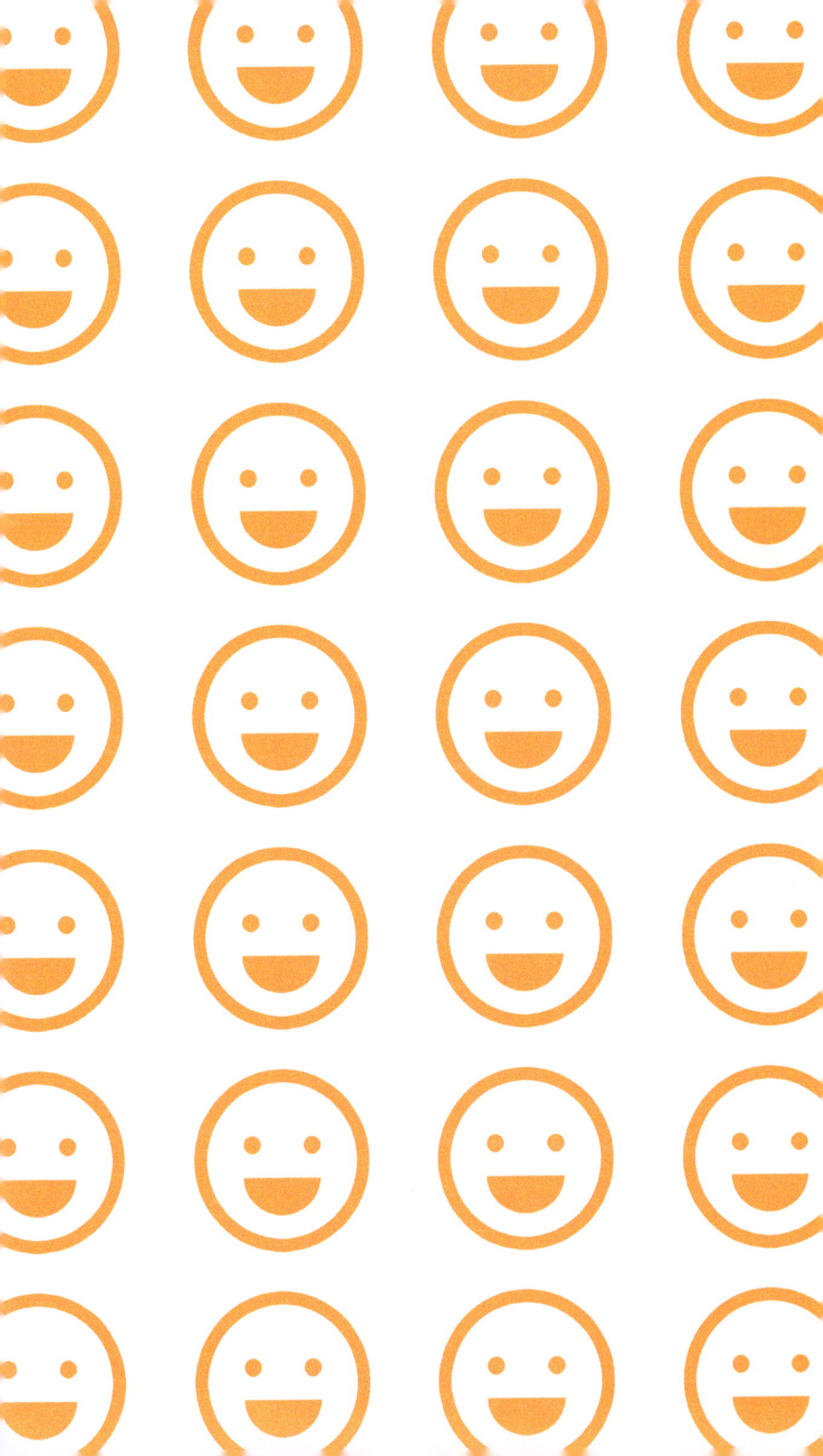

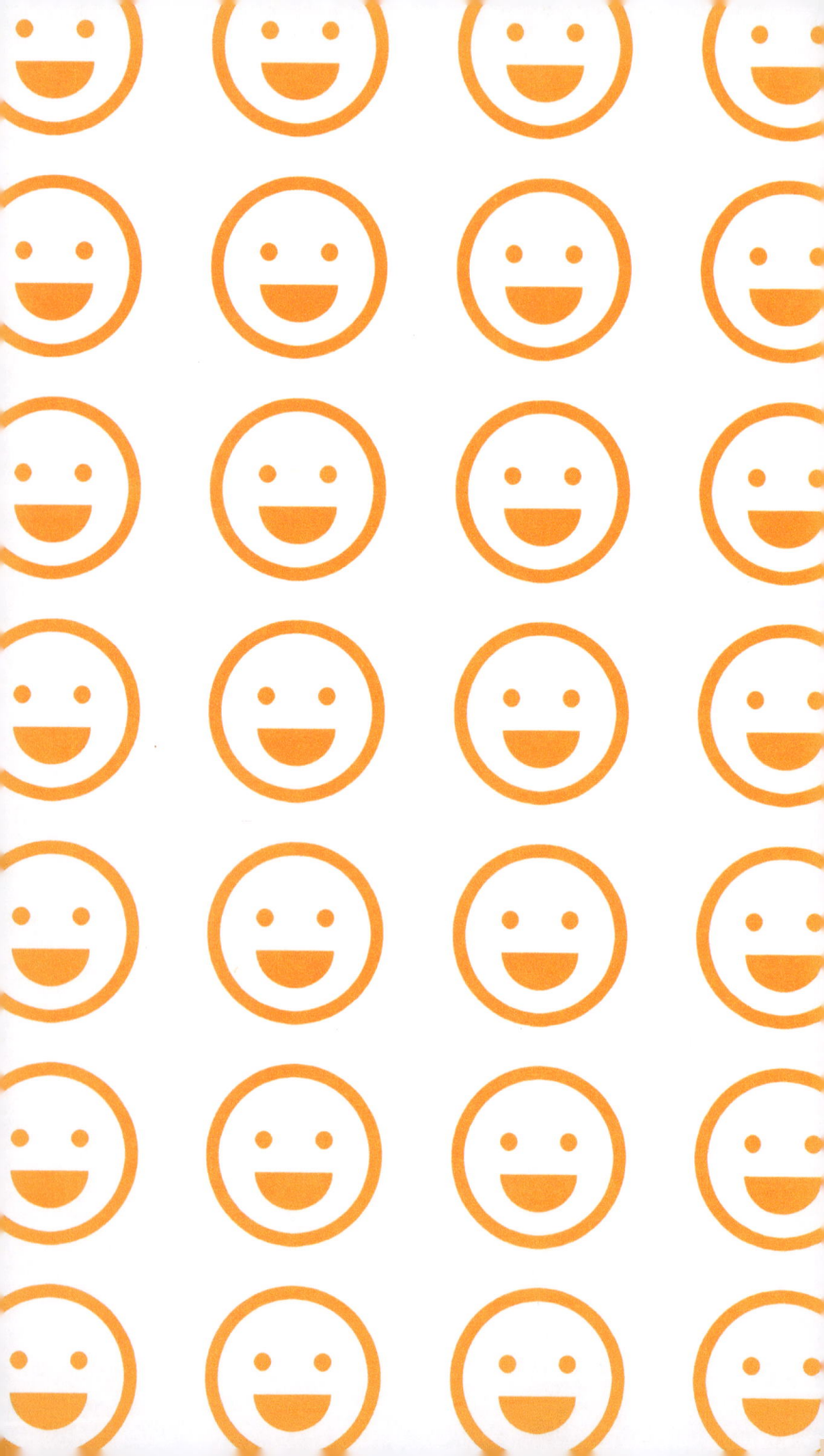

www.ingramcontent.com/pod-product-compliance
Lightning Source LLC
Chambersburg PA
CBHW041108280526
45792CB00010B/2342